BMX

BMX

ODYSSEYS

JIM WHITING

CREATIVE EDUCATION · CREATIVE PAPERBACKS

Published by Creative Education and Creative Paperbacks
P.O. Box 227, Mankato, Minnesota 56002
Creative Education and Creative Paperbacks
are imprints of The Creative Company
www.thecreativecompany.us

Design by Blue Design (www.bluedes.com)
Production by Joe Kahnke
Art direction by Rita Marshall
Printed in China

Photographs by Alamy (Simon Balson; Everett Collection, Inc.; Lumi Images; PA Images; ScreenProd/Photononstop), benscycle.com, Dreamstime (Mohamad Ridzuan Abdul Rashid), Flickr (Eli Christman, Ruben Lamers), Getty Images (Sam Adams/Aurora, Jonathan Daniel/Getty Images Sport, CARL DE SOUZA/AFP, Tim de Waele/Corbis Sport, Silver Screen Collection/Moviepix, ullstein bild Dtl./ullstein bild, Connor Walberg/Stone), iStockphoto (Pgiam), Newscom (CROSNIER/DPPI-SIPA), Shutterstock (ARENA Creative, homydesign, MarcelClemens)

Photograph on page 66 courtesy of Keith Mulligan.

Library of Congress Cataloging-in-Publication Data
Names: Whiting, Jim, author.
Title: BMX / Jim Whiting.
Series: Odysseys in extreme sports.
Includes bibliographical references and index.
Summary: An in-depth survey of the popular extreme sport of bicycle motocross, from its teenaged origins to its current Olympic presence, as well as its techniques, rules, records, and famous bikers.
Identifiers: LCCN 2015027867 / ISBN 978-1-60818-691-4 (hardcover) / ISBN 978-1-62832-287-3 (pbk) / ISBN 978-1-56660-727-8 (eBook)

Subjects: LCSH: 1. ESPN X-Games—Juvenile literature. 2. Bicycle motocross—Juvenile literature.
Classification: LCC GV1049.3.W48 2016 / DDC 796.6/22—dc23

CCSS: RI 8.1, 2, 3, 4, 5, 8, 10; RI 9-10.1, 2, 3, 4, 5, 8, 10; RI 11-12.1, 2, 3, 4, 5, 10; RST 6-8.1, 2, 5, 6, 10; RST 9-10.1, 2, 5, 6, 10; RST 11-12.1, 2, 5, 6, 10

First Edition HC 9 8 7 6 5 4 3 2 1
First Edition PBK 9 8 7 6 5 4 3 2 1

CONTENTS

Introduction

Soured on soccer? Fed up with football? Bored by baseball? Turned off by team sports? If so, extreme sports might be more to your liking. While there's not an exact definition of what makes a sport "extreme," the following characteristics (or at least most of them) seem to be common: a higher degree of risk despite use of protective gear, emphasis on achieving high speeds and/or

OPPOSITE: To participate in BMX races, riders must wear helmets, long-sleeved shirts, and long pants, but some also choose to sport gloves and goggles for additional protection.

heights, more likely to be performed alone or with a handful of friends, no issues with playing time as in team sports, stunts requiring substantial amounts of skill and practice, less emphasis on formal rules, and an **adrenaline** rush from physical exertion.

One of the most popular extreme sports is BMX, or "bicycle motocross." BMX is noted for its dual nature of speed and flashiness. Love going fast? Then you'll want to enter BMX races that feature lots of obstacles. Every second counts because most races finish in fewer than 60 seconds. Lose focus for even a moment and you're toast. Maybe doing tricks gives you a rush. If so, BMX freestyle is for you. The great thing is that you don't have to choose. One day you can train for racing. The next day, work on your bag of tricks.

Mimicking Motorcycles

When someone says the words "founding father," you probably think of people like George Washington. Not a teenager in a T-shirt and cutoff jeans. But many people consider the "founding father" of BMX to be 13-year-old Scot Breithaupt of Long Beach, California. Despite his young age, Breithaupt was a motorcycle rider for the Yamaha Motor Corporation.

Yamaha had taken advantage of exploding interest in motorcycle riding in the United States that began during the 1950s and '60s. This growth was fueled in part by films such as *The Wild One* (1953) and the World War II-based *The Great Escape* (1963). One **offshoot** of this interest was the sport of motocross, which involved motorcycles careening at high speed around rough dirt tracks laden with obstacles and jumps.

Young people watched the excitement of motocross in person or on television and wanted a piece of the action. They were too young and too small to handle high-powered motorcycles, but they had a perfect substitute: the Schwinn Sting-Ray. In 1962, Schwinn bicycle engineer Al Fritz realized that many young riders were **retrofitting** their bikes with motorcycle components such as **ape-hanger handlebars** and banana seats. He designed

an entirely new bike with 20-inch-diameter (50.8 cm) wheels that incorporated these components. After a slow start, the Sting-Ray—and similar bikes by other manufacturers—soon became immensely popular. Even though kids couldn't ride a motorcycle, at least they had something that *looked* like one. The Sting-Ray's small size lent itself to doing tricks such as wheelies.

Breithaupt provided a focus for these Sting-Ray riders. He began attracting a crowd of onlookers at the dirt lot where he honed his motorcycle skills. "When I practiced, local kids would come out and imitate my jumps," he explained. "One day [in November 1970], I went home, got some of my motorcycle trophies and had the 35 kids there each pitch in a quarter. Broke them down into skill classes: beginner, **novice**, and expert. It was kewl, the next week 150 kids showed up!" They kept

coming, and word quickly spread throughout Southern California about this great new sport. Breithaupt helped set up tracks in neighboring communities. Within a few years, entries in these races routinely topped 1,000. In 1974, the Los Angeles Coliseum hosted the finals of the Yamaha Bicycle Gold Cup series, established and promoted by Breithaupt.

I n the meantime, BMX had gone "national" in 1971, thanks to the motorcycle film *On Any Sunday*. Now that more kids were becoming involved, the bikes themselves and supporting equipment began improving as well. Publications such as *BMX Action*, which began in 1976, helped spread the word.

Up to this point, BMX had largely been devoted to racing. Later in the 1970s, riders began realizing that their bikes were ideally sized to do tricks. One of the trendsetters was Bob Haro, who became known as the "Godfather of Freestyle." In addition to pioneering many stunts, in the early 1980s, he built new bike frames especially suited to doing tricks.

Not long afterward, riders began utilizing **half-pipes** and **quarter-pipes**, which gave rise to vert freestyling. Riders would approach the ramps with as much speed as possible. Then they would soar into the air and do tricks. Daredevils such as Dave Mirra and Mat Hoffman kept pushing the envelope, both in terms of the incredible heights they attained and the spectacular

tricks they did in midair.

BMX riding—and other extreme sports—received a huge boost in 1995 with the new X Games. Created especially for television by the ESPN network, the X Games attracted large numbers of young viewers. BMX was one of nine sports selected for the inaugural competition. Riders welcomed the event, but they were wary of being perceived as little more than a circus act. Steve Swope, both a competing pro and a BMX event organizer, told *BMX Business News* several years later, "We all knew it was going to be the biggest BMX competition ever and hopefully it would be done with minimal cheesiness and represented us in as close to true form as TV is capable. It came off very well." The first X Games featured two BMX events. Today, spectators are treated to five, a reflection of the increasing popularity of the sport.

The sport reached its pinnacle when it was included in the 2008 Summer Olympic Games in Beijing, China. Maris Strombergs of Latvia topped 31 other competitors from 20 countries for the men's gold medal. Americans Mike Day and Donny Robinson took home silver and bronze respectively. In the women's race, Anne-Caroline Chausson of France took the gold. Jill Kintner of the U.S. wove her way through a couple of crashes to capture the bronze medal.

Recognizing the continuing interest in BMX, organizers of the next Olympics in London, England, in 2012 planned and rehearsed a five-minute stunt sequence during the Opening Ceremonies. But it had to be cut at the last moment because of time constraints.

On the track, Strombergs defended his title, while Mariana Pajón of Colombia led the women. Sam Willoughby of Australia and Carlos Oquendo Zabala of Colombia took the other two men's medals. New Zealand's Sarah Walker was the women's silver medalist, with Laura Smulders of the Netherlands taking bronze. Americans were shut out of the medals, as Connor Fields was seventh in the men's final, while countrywoman Brooke Crain finished eighth in the women's final. Sixteen other nations had entrants.

Such geographical diversity proves that a sport originating in a few vacant lots in Southern California just a few decades earlier has now become a worldwide phenomenon. And this phenomenon shows no signs of slackening.

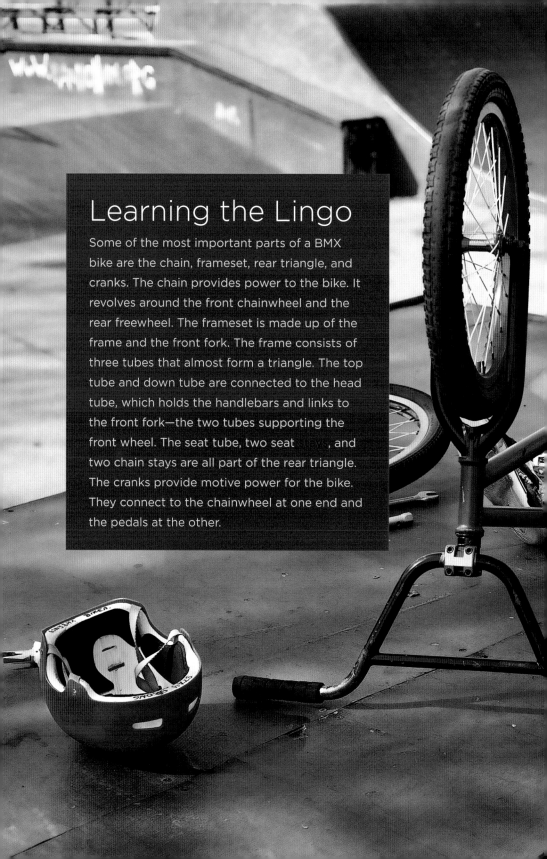

Learning the Lingo

Some of the most important parts of a BMX bike are the chain, frameset, rear triangle, and cranks. The chain provides power to the bike. It revolves around the front chainwheel and the rear freewheel. The frameset is made up of the frame and the front fork. The frame consists of three tubes that almost form a triangle. The top tube and down tube are connected to the head tube, which holds the handlebars and links to the front fork—the two tubes supporting the front wheel. The seat tube, two seat stays, and two chain stays are all part of the rear triangle. The cranks provide motive power for the bike. They connect to the chainwheel at one end and the pedals at the other.

Buying and Riding a BMX

The most essential part of BMX riding is the bike itself. There are many factors to consider in making a purchase. Online buying guides from trusted sources are helpful to consult. So are salespeople at bike shops, who often have advice based on personal experience.

Once you have picked out a bike, the next consideration is protective gear. Most important is a helmet.

OPPOSITE: BMX bicycles come in different sizes and weights; a lightweight bike is easier to control and allows the user to ride for a longer time before getting tired.

Types of BMX Bikes

According to experts, BMX bikes are divided into three categories: "True" BMX are intended for racing. They are lighter than the other two, and the more money you spend, the less they weigh. They have knobbed tires for gaining traction. They have only rear brakes, as squeezing a front brake to make a sudden stop could catapult a rider over the handlebars. Lightweight wheels help accelerate out of the starting gate. Freestyle bikes have heavier frames and wheels because they bear more pounding from landing jumps. Front and rear brakes provide maximum flexibility for tricks. They may have axle pegs to stand on during stunts. Dirt jumpers are a combination of true BMX and freestyle

While it is sometimes jokingly referred to as a "brain bucket," there's nothing funny about tumbling head first off your bike. You'll want full-face protection to minimize the chance of injury. A tinted visor improves vision in direct sunlight. Goggles will protect your eyes from all the dirt that's kicked up during races.

A heavy, long-sleeved shirt and pants that fit tightly around the ankles are also vital. Keep your joints from serious injury with knee and elbow pads. Gloves prevent painful scrapes and cuts on your hands if you fall off. When you get really involved in the sport, specially designed BMX shoes can be a good investment. You'll also want padding on several parts of your bike.

With your bike and safety gear in place, you're ready to head for a track. Tracks can be indoors or outdoors. Indoor tracks are often shorter because of space constraints.

The most common lengths range from about 900 feet (274 m) to 1,300 feet (396 m). They vary in width from about 30 feet (9.1 m) at the start to a narrower 10 feet (3 m) at some points along the course.

They are packed with obstacles, such as hills. Some hills are relatively high and can send riders soaring several feet off the track. But the longer a rider is in the air, the more time it takes to finish. For a sport in which tiny fractions of a second are important, such airtime can be costly. Courses may also include a series of smaller hills called whoop-de-dos. And any time you are airborne, the trick when landing is to come down on the rear wheel. Landing on the front wheel could catapult you over the handlebars!

All tracks have several turns. One type is a berm, a high-speed turn with a high bank on the outside. Esse turns require riders to quickly swerve in one direction and then back in the opposite direction, like the letter S. Flat turns have no bank and are the likeliest to cause crashes. There may even be water or mud jumps. The course ends with a straight and flat stretch, which allows riders to pump their pedals furiously to the finish line.

Anywhere from two to eight riders start a race with their bikes poised at the top of a steep ramp. Lights on the starting gate flash red-yellow-yellow-green. The gate drops and you're off! You must stay in your lane until the bottom of the ramp. Clearly, there's an advantage to taking the lead right away, as other racers must try to pass the leader. In such tight spaces there's a good chance of crashing. Riders may remount after a crash, but their chance of winning is diminished. Many BMX races begin with a series of three heats. Riders receive points

Riders who participate in the national championship race in their home country can qualify for the BMX World Championships, which are organized by Union Cycliste Internationale and held in a different location each year.

based on where they finish. First gets one point, second two points, and so on. Those with the lowest point totals advance to the finals. The finals often consist of another series of three races, though sometimes—such as in the Olympics—it's a single winner-take-all race.

BMX freestyle can be just as appealing—and fun—as racing. It comes in five forms: dirt jumping, street riding, flatland, park riding, and vert. Dirt jumping reflects the sport's origins. Riders jump from one dirt mound—about five feet (1.5 m) high—to another and try

to perform a trick in midair. These mounds are often put at the bottom of a slight decline to allow riders to build up more speed and thereby rise especially high.

In street riding, riders utilize public streets and whatever obstacles they encounter, such as curbs, benches, and stairs. Such environments make this the most dangerous form of freestyle. Even quiet streets can quickly become dangerous with the sudden appearance of a vehicle. And approaching an obstacle at high speed without knowing what lies on the other side can lead to accidents.

Flatland riders use large paved surfaces such as parking lots to perform tricks without ramps or obstacles. Instead, they often depend on balance as they spin and twirl. Many flatland bikes are equipped with pegs that riders use to stand on during their tricks.

With the increasing popularity of both skateboarding

With the increasing popularity of both skateboarding and BMX, specially designed skateparks are cropping up all over the U.S.

and BMX, specially designed skateparks are cropping up all over the U.S. Park riders use these parks and ramps for their tricks.

Vert is an offshoot of park riding. Riders zip up half-pipes and quarter-pipes—usually around 10 feet (3 m) high—that end in a vertical wall. They perform a midair trick, and then land back on the ramp.

Regardless of the variation, experts maintain that it's important to visualize the trick before you start. They say you need to relax and form a mental image of the entire trick: starting from a dead stop, progressing through each stage, and ending with its completion.

Most beginning BMXers start with "ground tricks." These are relatively easy to master and don't involve

the risk of serious injury. One such trick is the wheelie. Riders shift their weight backward to make the front wheel come off the ground. Good riders can maintain this position for considerable lengths of time. An endo is the opposite maneuver, balancing the bike on the front tire. Kick turns are another trick. To execute a kick turn, ride to the top of a short hill. Stop with the front wheel off the ground, and then snap the bike in a 180-degree turn and return to the bottom of the hill. Pogoing involves hopping forward on one tire, while sidewalking is hopping to the side. Bunny-hopping is a series of forward bounces with both wheels off the ground at the same time.

Once you're comfortable with these tricks, you can progress to more complicated maneuvers. Who knows how far—or high—you can go?

Jump Up!

One of the first skills riders need to acquire is jumping. Approaching the ramp, you need to gain as much speed as possible. That means starting a good distance away and pedaling as fast as you can. When you're about 15 to 30 feet (4.6–9.1 m) from the base of the ramp, drop into a bunny-hop position, with your knees and elbows bent. (Visualize yourself as a coiled spring.) At the top of ramp, pull your front wheel up. Then, as your back wheel hits the top, try to "uncoil" and even out your bike so that it's level. Land with your front wheel down and squat back to prevent yourself from flipping over the handlebars. Keep practicing until all the movements become automatic.

Pioneers of Big Air and Olympic Medals

Though Bob Haro was a relative latecomer to BMX, starting at the age of 18 after years of motorcycle racing, he quickly made a name for himself for the tricks he invented. "I was like the first guy that could do 360s on a jump, roll backs, coaster wheelies—everyone was just blown away. I was like an instant hero," he said. Soon afterward he formed the country's first freestyle trick team.

In 1981, Haro and fellow trick team member Bob Morales undertook an 18,000-mile (28,968 km), 3-month tour of the U.S. to promote freestyling. During the long hours on the road, Haro conceived the idea of a new frame and fork designed specifically for freestyle. The following year, his company began producing the now-legendary Haro Freestyler. Haro has remained active in the sport ever since.

In recognition of his accomplishments, Haro was selected to **choreograph** a segment of the Opening Ceremony of the 2012 Summer Olympics. Seventy-five riders, each wearing a pair of flapping dove wings, rode around the track in one of the most memorable parts of the production.

One of the beneficiaries of Haro's efforts was Mat "The Condor" Hoffman, who began his competitive freestyle career in 1985 at the age of 13. The soaring nickname is especially fitting for the man also known as the "Father of Big Air" because of his high-flying accomplishments. "He was the first guy to do any sort of big ramp stuff," said legendary skateboarder Tony Hawk. "Now we've got the whole Big Air event in the X Games, and that's largely because of Mat ever trying it or ever dreaming of it."

Hoffman began building his legend in 1990 when he assembled a 21-foot (6.4 m) quarter-pipe—twice the usual size—and had a motorcycle tow him to it at speeds of up to 50 miles (80.5 km) per hour. At first, people thought photos that documented the event had to be fakes. A live public demonstration soon proved they weren't.

Despite the inevitable crashes (Hoffman has had more than two dozen operations and suffered a ruptured

spleen), he keeps pushing the altitude envelope. "You hit the peak of it and you're centered and you're in control and you feel like you're flying, like you're floating on top of the world," Hoffman says of his big-air exploits. "It makes me glow until I'm the most alive I've ever been."

Hoffman is also responsible for the development of more than 100 tricks. Perhaps the most notable is the no-handed 900, in which the rider does two and a half loops while airborne and briefly takes his hands off the handlebars.

Dave Mirra helped Hoffman put BMX firmly into the public consciousness. He started street riding at the age of four with his older brother. Six years later, he entered his first race. He was second to last. He turned his attention to freestyle and quickly attained success. Many BMX fans believed that he could surpass Hoffman as the top

vert rider by the time he graduated from high school. At the age of 19, though, he was hit by a car. Mirra suffered a broken shoulder and a blood clot in his brain. Doctors warned him that another blow to his head could lead to death. But Mirra was determined to keep riding. Within six months, he was back on his bike, and soon ascended to the top levels of the sport. Before his death in 2016, he had won 14 gold medals in the X Games.

While Hoffman, Mirra, and others were making headlines for going up and down, the inclusion of BMX in the 2008 Olympics focused attention on going as fast as possible. One of the most notable entries was Jill Kintner of the U.S. Like many youngsters, she took up BMX at a young age. "I was the only girl in our neighborhood, and I would go on these bike missions with the boys all the time," she explains on her website.

She turned to serious racing when she was just 14 years old. Seeking new challenges after winning national and world championships by the time she was 21, she turned to mountain biking and added new hardware to her trophy case.

Even after learning that BMX would be part of the Summer Olympics in 2008, Kintner was hesitant to return to the sport. "It's easy to switch from a BMX bike to a mountain bike, but it's tricky to go the other way," she points out. "Mountain bikes are more stable and roll smoother; you can hit jumps without being perfect, but on a BMX bike you have to be perfect."

Persuaded to try out, she suffered a serious knee injury late in 2007 and reinjured it the following April. Aided by a knee brace, she gritted her way through the team selection process, qualified for the Games, and

won a bronze medal.

On the men's side in the Olympics, Maris Strombergs of Latvia proved to be the biggest name, though his BMX career got off to a rocky start. "I was five years old when my father took me to the BMX track, and when I saw all those big guys jumping those big doubles, I started crying. I said, 'No way, Dad.'"

His father was persistent. Four years after Strombergs decided to give the sport a try, he won his age group at the world championships. He maintained that high level of racing and became the first male BMX Summer Olympic gold medalist in 2008. He jumped off to a quick start in the final and led from start to finish. Based on that impressive win and his imposing physical stature—6-foot-1 and nearly 200 pounds—he acquired the nickname of "The Latvian Machine."

He returned to the Olympics in 2012 as the heavy favorite but finished sixth in the semifinals. The finals were a different story. Strombergs surged into the lead right away and maintained his edge to the finish. Many fans expected a three-peat in the 2016 Games in Rio de Janeiro, Brazil. Unfortunately, a hard crash in his first run kept Strombergs out of medal contention as he failed to qualify for the finals.

Maris "The Latvian Machine" Strombergs is the only person from his country to win more than one Olympic gold medal in an individual event.

BMX on the Big Screen and in Books

One of the earliest media depictions of motocross came in the 1963 film *The Great Escape*. American pilot Virgil "The Cooler King" Hilts (played by Steve McQueen) tries to escape from a German prison camp during World War II on a stolen motorcycle. An accomplished rider, McQueen insisted on doing most of his own stunts. (Though, for insurance reasons, stuntman Bud Ekins performed the most famous jump over a barbed-wire fence.) McQueen's off-road motorcycle escapade gave moviegoers of the '60s a taste for what would become BMX.

t also inspired filmmakers such as director Bruce Brown. Brown said he was so stoked after seeing *The Great Escape* that he bought his first motor-cycle. He and McQueen became good friends, and the actor helped finance the 1971 film *On Any Sunday*. He also appeared in some of the scenes. With the filming

Steve McQueen's work in *The Great Escape* sparked nationwide interest in motorcycles and led to increased sales, which ultimately caused manufacturers to produce bicycles that looked more like motorcycles as well.

of *On Any Sunday*, Brown, who had already made the classic surfing movie *Endless Summer* in 1966, created what many critics call the most important documentary about motorcycle racers. Roger Ebert, for example, noted, "Brown sees them as basically having fun." It was nominated for an Oscar in the Best Documentary Feature category.

The opening credits of the film feature an early BMX race in a vacant lot in Southern California. Eight boys, each mounted on a Sting-Ray, pedal furiously to the accompaniment of motorcycle sounds. Almost immediately, they hit a bump and soar several feet into the air. They are not wearing helmets or other safety gear—just T-shirts, jeans, and tennis shoes. Going down an incline, one boy slips off his seat, runs beside his bike while holding on to the handlebars, then remounts. He wins the race. Then we see the same boy, now shirtless, doing a wheelie on a street for several blocks.

Kids in darkened theaters watching the film with their parents were hooked. Many people believe that this scene—which lasted just a minute and a half—did for youngsters what the rest of the film did for motorcycle racing by creating the excitement of racing and demonstrating a basic trick.

hree films in the 1980s helped fuel the increasing interest in BMX. In 1982, *E.T. the Extraterrestrial* was

Riding to the Moon

The 1982 movie *E.T. the Extraterrestrial* features a BMX chase scene in which the young hero Elliott and four friends elude police using their riding skills. Just as all seems lost, they rise into the air and soar above the suburban landscape before coming down in a forest. Elliott and E.T. soon are airborne again. The film's signature moment then occurs as Elliott, E.T., and the bike are silhouetted against the full moon. Millions of young viewers saw riding BMX bikes as a means of escaping parental restrictions, giving them a sense of freedom. Perhaps the only downside is that the eight young BMX riders who performed the stunts didn't receive recognition in the end credits.

released, and the final part of the film depicted the hero Elliott using his BMX bike to help E.T. go home. The film had a particularly strong impact on a Scottish boy named Chris Hoy. "I was watching *E.T.* when I was six years of age. I'd never seen a BMX bike before, and it was the scene at the end where they are getting chased by the police and they're all hammering through the streets in their BMX bikes. And I just thought, 'Wow, I'd like to give that a go.'" The only difference between Hoy and millions of other youngsters is that Hoy raced BMX professionally for seven years. Then he switched to road and track bicycles and won 11 world titles and 6 Olympic gold medals.

The Australian film *BMX Bandits* (1983) features actress Nicole Kidman in one of her first roles. Her character, Judy, and two buddies want to earn enough money to buy new BMX bikes and develop a race course. Their efforts run afoul of a gang, thereby providing the opportunity for numerous stunts, including a ride down a water slide.

Released three years later, *Rad* depicts the efforts of Cru Jones (played by Bill Allen) to overcome obstacles and compete in Helltrack, a prestigious BMX race, with the aid of his girlfriend, an amateur racer named Christian (Lori Loughlin). Former Olympic gold-medal-winning gymnast Bart Conner plays Bart Taylor, a factory racer who is Cru's primary rival. A number of top riders played themselves, which no doubt helped the stunts and racing scenes seem especially realistic. In 2015, *Heroes of Dirt* features a self-centered, would-be BMX pro named Phin Cooper (Joel Moody). Briefly jailed for unpaid traffic tickets, Cooper is released to perform community service

THRILLS,
CHILLS, SPILLS!
LIVE THE POWER OF THE...

BMX BANDITS

COMWORLD PRESENTS

A FILM BY BRIAN TRENCHARD-SMITH

BMX BANDITS

STARRING **DAVID ARGUE, JOHN LEY, NICOLE KIDMAN, ANGELO D'ANGELO, JAMES LUGTON**
DIRECTOR: **BRIAN TRENCHARD-SMITH**   DIRECTOR OF PHOTOGRAPHY: **JOHN SEALE, A.S.C.**
SCREENPLAY: **PATRICK EDGEWORTH** BASED ON A SCREENPLAY BY: **RUSSELL HAGG**
MUSIC: **COLIN STEAD AND FRANK STRANGIO** ASSOCIATE PRODUCER: **BRIAN D. BURGESS**

PRODUCERS: **TOM BROADBRIDGE & PAUL F. DAVIES**

FILMED IN PANAVISION®   󰀀󰀀 DOLBY STEREO™

by mentoring a teenager. The two bond over riding, and the film is especially notable for a dazzling array of tricks.

In 2000, the first BMX video game was released. Called *Dave Mirra Freestyle BMX*, it was followed by *Dave Mirra Freestyle BMX 2* in 2001. Those two games have since been joined by a host of others for PlayStation, Xbox, and other formats.

In addition to dozens of technique books for riders of all levels, a number of fictional works target young readers. These include a series called Jake Maddox Sports Stories. In *BMX Challenge* (2011), a character named Jason accepts a dare to take part in a BMX competition despite his inexperience in the sport. *BMX Bully* (2007) features Matt, whose chances of earning a slot on a racing team are threatened by a cheating newcomer.

Sports Illustrated magazine has a series of sports-themed graphic novels. In *BMX Breakthrough* (2012) by Carl Bowen, a daredevil named Billy Cruz tries to recover from a serious bike accident. A major BMX race portrays three of the state's top riders on the eve of competing on a super-secret course—but one of them seems to have advance knowledge—in *BMX Blitz* (2011) by Scott Ciencin.

Author Adie Copping takes a different tack in *Tommy Treadwood: The BMX Hero* (2013). Tommy is a klutz who acquires magical powers that enable him to perform a spectacular series of tricks. In his spare time, he and his best friend Barney do a bit of crime solving. *On the Gate* (2015), by Richard Wielkiewicz, chronicles the adventures and challenges of BMX rider Nate Walker as he moves up from the novice classification to intermediate.

Race to the Future

What lies ahead for BMX? As was the case in the beginning, media exposure plays a key role in its growth and development. Both racing and freestyle benefit from putting viewers up close and personal to the action. As bicycle reviewer Saris Mercanti noted just before the 2012 Olympics, "The sport of BMX racing is incredibly engaging for millions of viewers who don't understand the subtleties of road racing. Instead of being subjected

OPPOSITE: BMX racing appeals to a wide range of people; there are events for all ages, even very young children, and families can practice together.

Sidehacks

Some riders like to add a sidehack, a platform with a single wheel that is connected to the bike. A passenger—known as a "monkey"—stands or crouches on the platform while clutching a grip extending across its width. Sidehacks are normally used for street riding and racing, though it's possible to do some tricks with them as well. The monkey isn't just along for the ride. He or she has several important functions: jumping off at the base of hills and helping to push the bike upward, shifting weight around curves, helping balance the bike/sidehack on two wheels, and more. To accommodate the extra weight of the monkey, the sidehack wheel is usually heavier than the other two. Installation is often as simple as attaching a few bolts to the bike.

to an hour's long race filled with tightly packed spandex-clad athletes, a BMX race is over in just a few tense minutes, and features gigantic doubles and sweeping berms." Viewers from around the globe tuned in to watch the world's top-rated racers compete against each other in 2012, and it's likely that many of them wanted to emulate that action when they turned off their televisions.

The same holds true for the boost freestyle has received from telecasts of the X Games. As the event becomes even more popular, the prize money for competitors also increases, making the top names both more willing to show off their skills and to push the envelope of the difficulty level of their tricks. This creates even more spectator interest and a desire to take up the sport.

There can be little doubt of the continuing popularity of the X Games. In 2014, a new venue was chosen. The

Circle of the Americas (COTA) sports and entertainment complex in Austin, Texas, was selected as the future site of the games. "We believe that [COTA founder] Bobby Epstein, his team, and the fantastic COTA facility provide a unique opportunity to grow the X Games in a new region of the country and in a city that has a proven track record of embracing big events," said Scott Guglielmo of ESPN. "Ultimately, the combination of resources, support, and fit brought us to Austin, and we couldn't be happier."

The growing participation in the X Games, along with the number of nations represented in the Olympic-level BMX competition, reflect the ongoing international growth of the sport. In England, for example, British rider/coach Nathaniel Martin noted, "It's so different from when I was growing up; it's improved so much over the past 5 to 10 years. The Olympics has really helped. We have more Go-Ride BMX clubs and tracks than ever before, which gives more opportunities for new and existing riders to try out the sport in a safe environment."

The situation is much the same in Australia, which bills itself as having the second-largest BMX industry in the world. Mark Lewis, general manager of BMX Australia, the sport's governing organization, said in the group's 2013 annual report that "BMX Australia has seen a significant increase across the board in memberships to 14,481, which is a 75 percent increase on 2012 figures." The following year, he added, "BMX Australia continues to see consistent membership growth with membership now sitting just under 17,000. This continued growth is an indicator that the sport of BMX is something that both children and families can relate to. The data suggests that boys and girls aged 2–20 years have found BMX an appealing and engaging sport."

One key development has been the expansion of the age range of riders. The sport is becoming increasingly popular among children who have only recently begun to walk. Wearing specially designed protective gear and riding smaller-scaled bikes with wheels as small as 12 inches (30.5 cm) across, they gain an early introduction to the sport that their older siblings continue to pursue so happily. A few bikes are even the "strider" type, featuring BMX-style frames and wheels but no pedals.

Becoming involved at an early age provides an attachment to the sport that often makes riders more committed and not as easily turned away as they grow older. Many longtime BMX stars remain active in the sport, even if they no longer compete in events.

It also helps that many towns and cities are constructing skateparks to give BMX riders safe locations to practice their skills. In addition, YouTube and other media sites cover every aspect of the sport, from extreme tricks and racing to buyers' guides.

BMX is becoming an increasingly attractive alternative to traditional sports. While soccer, baseball, basketball, and others will always have many participants, they do have a few shortcomings: well-documented examples of parents attacking other parents, coaches, game officials, and even youthful participants; significant injuries such as concussions and broken bones; and inflexible practice times that may involve penalties if a player cannot attend. While BMX carries its own injury risks (which can be reduced by wearing the proper protective gear), riders usually have the luxury of practicing when it best fits

As an increasing number of communities construct skateparks and BMX tracks, more riders are able to try out this ever-growing sport.

their schedules.

As the sport continues to gain popularity, event opportunities also multiply. For example, a new form of racing called Double Cross is likely to add interest to the sport. The format is simple: two riders go head-to-head over a series of high dirt jumps. Several heats narrow the original field until the final pair races for the championship.

Speaking about Double Cross, pro rider Derek Sipkoi, owner and founder of Dkoi Bikes, said, "I was just welcomed to a completely new exciting format for BMX and I had the time of my life ... The only expressions to be seen from the participants was an overwhelming smile of joy.... This can be a direction the BMX community can leap towards, and truly bring back a passion to the roots of our shared sport, BICYCLE MOTO X!!!"

BMX has come a long way since its early days. Advances in bike technology have pushed the envelope in terms of speed and height. Increases in competitive opportunities, such as indoor tracks with a full array of obstacles, attract new and seasoned racers. As a result, riders of all ages continually push their personal limits and rise to a level of performance they may have never believed they could attain.

Glossary

adrenaline   a substance produced by the body, often when physically or emotionally stressed, characterized by increased blood flow and heightened excitement

ape-hanger handlebars   especially high, angled handlebars

choreograph   compose the sequence of moves for a performance

half-pipes   ramps with two surfaces facing each other that curve inward, equivalent to half of a round pipe

novice   a person new to an activity, with no previous experience

offshoot   something that originates from something else and develops in its own way

quarter-pipes   ramps with a surface that curves inward, equivalent to one-fourth of a round pipe

retrofitting   adding something to a product that wasn't originally part of it when it was manufactured

spleen	an organ located near the stomach that is involved in the production and removal of blood cells
stays	thin, usually tapered tubes that connect two parts of a bike frame

Selected Bibliography

Donaldson, Tony. *BMX Trix and Techniques for the Park and Street*. Osceola, Wis.: Motorbooks International, 2004.

Hon, Shek. *BMX Riding Skills: The Guide to Flatland Tricks*. New York: Firefly Books, 2010.

Jeffries, Tom, and Ian Thewlis. *BMX Racing*. Ramsbury, Wiltshire, UK: Crowood Press, 2013.

Kaelberer, Angie Peterson. *BMX Racing*. North Mankato, Minn.: Capstone Press, 2006.

Lucas, Gavin, and Stuart Robinson. *Rad Rides: The Best BMX Bikes of All Time*. London: Laurence King, 2012.

Maurer, Tracy Nelson. *BMX Freestyle*. Vero Beach, Fla.: Rourke, 2002.

McCormack, Lee. *Pro BMX Skills: Equipment, Techniques, Tactics, and Training*. Boulder, Colo.: Race Line, 2010.

Polydoros, Lori. *Awesome Freestyle BMX Tricks & Stunts*. North Mankato, Minn.: Capstone Press, 2011.

Websites

Ride BMX: 10 Tips for Buying a Complete BMX Bike

*https://www.ridebmx.com/features/10-tips-for-buying-a
-complete-bmx-bike/*

This is an illustrated overview of the most important elements in making an informed buying decision, presented in a somewhat irreverent yet authoritative tone. Links at the end provide additional resources.

USA BMX: The American Bicycle Assocation

http://www.usabmx.com/#&slider1=1

This site offers news, photos, results, a list of local certified coaches, and a listing of more than 370 tracks with event schedules, driving directions, and more.

Note: Every effort has been made to ensure that any websites listed above were active at the time of publication. However, because of the nature of the Internet, it is impossible to guarantee that these sites will remain active indefinitely or that their contents will not be altered.

Index